# Vintage Revised
# Jewelry

# Vintage Revised
# Jewelry

35 step-by-step projects inspired by lost,
found, and recycled treasures

*Co-Co Nichole Bush

CICO BOOKS
LONDON NEW YORK

Published in 2013 by CICO Books

An imprint of Ryland Peters & Small

519 Broadway, 5th Floor,
New York NY 10012

20–21 Jockey's Fields,
London WC1R 4BW

www.cicobooks.com

10 9 8 7 6 5 4 3 2 1

A CIP catalog record for this book is
available from the Library of
Congress and the British Library.

ISBN: 978-1-908862-70-9

Printed in China

Editor: Sarah Hoggett
Designer: Barbara Zuñiga
Illustrator: Michael A. Hill
Photographer: Gavin Kingcome
Stylist: Luis Peral-Aranda

# Contents

# Introduction

I enjoy finding quirky, memorable, and soulful treasures that I can transform into something new. I have a passion for making one-of-a-kind jewelry from antique and vintage pieces. I love to use pieces that tell a story or create one once it's designed. I usually don't have a plan in advance—but I will know it when I see it!

For me, one of the passions of incorporating vintage elements into my jewelry designs is that they open a window on the past. Sometimes, the item itself may have belonged to someone dear to me; even an inexpensive, broken piece of costume jewelry takes on special meaning because I know that it was once worn by someone I love. At other times, it's more an association of ideas: a watch fob (even a modern one from the scrapbooking section of a crafts store) might trigger thoughts of ancestors long since departed, a broken key can hint at a secret that was once behind locked pages of a diary, buttons from a favorite shirt remind you of your child.

However, I don't want to just copy old jewelry designs. I want to create something that has a contemporary edge to it, something that combines the old with the new, the nostalgic with the quirky, fun side of my personality—so I also look for things that will give my jewelry a twist. They don't even have to be designed specifically for jewelry: in this book, you'll find things as diverse as bits of old chain, keyhole covers from my local home improvements store, even brass tags and

industrial labels. I choose them for their hidden meanings and associations, and also for their shape, color, and texture, and because I know they will either contrast with or complement the vintage elements.

The aim of this book is to show you how you, too, can create unique pieces of jewelry by repurposing, recycling, and revising aged materials and giving them new life. It is designed for ages 9–99 and for all skill levels. It takes you on 35 journeys, step by step, teaching you techniques and giving you ideas that you can duplicate, build on, or imitate in your own way. I don't want this to be another book that you put on your shelf and just take out to look at the pictures from time to time—it's not for that! Use it as a tool to learn new skills, enhance the ones you already have, and inspire you.

You can expect to spend hours of enjoyment, days of treasure hunting, weeks of creating, and years of giving your own personal designs to friends and family. Your creations will not look exactly like the ones shown here, because your own heirlooms and found "treasures" will be different and you will need to find your own ways to showcase them and give them new life. But I hope that my jewelry will spark off ideas in you and that, every time you open the book, you will find a new design concept to awaken your creative soul.

*Co-Co Bush
(aka Kyler's Mom)

# Tools

Here are my suggestions for a basic tool kit that every jewelry maker should have; occasionally I use other, more specialized, pieces of equipment, but I've included a list of tools with each project in this book so that you can check you've got everything you need before you start.

**Beading mat (not shown)**
This is a great piece of equipment to have to hand, as you can lay out the components of your piece of jewelry in order and they will not roll around.

**Wire cutters**
There are several kinds of wire cutter on the market, but I find that "side cutters" are the most useful because the small, tapered blades can cut into small spaces.

**Pliers**
From top to bottom: Round-, flat-, and chain-nose pliers. Round-nose pliers have round, tapered shafts and are used to curl wire into a loop. Flat- and chain-nose pliers are used to grip wire and other pieces firmly as you work.

**Hammer and steel block**
Specialty jewelry hammers are smaller and lighter than general-purpose household hammers, but you can use any hammer as long as one end has a flat, smooth surface. Steel blocks can be bought from specialty jewelry stores, but any flat, smooth steel surface will do.

**Dremel tool**
Dremel tools usually have an assortment of interchangeable heads so you can use them for a variety of tasks, from cutting away unwanted metal and drilling holes to sanding and polishing.

**Drill**
A small electric drill is essential for drilling holes in metal or other hard surfaces. When you're using a drill, place the piece you're drilling into on a wooden block.

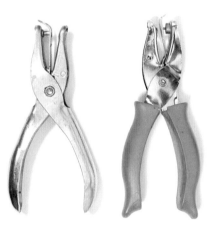

**Center punch**
Use a center punch to create an indentation before drilling a hole so that the bit doesn't slip when you start to drill.

**Hole punches**
There are several different types available, from those that are specifically made to punch through metal to those that are general purpose or designed for fabric such as leather. Some are adjustable, enabling you to punch holes of different diameters.

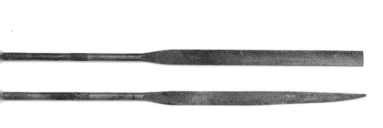

**Files**
Files come in different sizes and shapes and are useful for smoothing the edges of sawn metal. The two files that I use most often are the flat hand file and the half round—useful in sanding rounded areas. Smaller needle files are very useful for detail work.

**Tweezers**
Small tweezers are invaluable for positioning tiny decorative items such as crystals.

# Materials

When it comes to making imaginative, one-of-a-kind pieces of jewelry, anything goes! Some things—beads and jewelry chains (both new and recycled from broken pieces), and ready-made findings such as ear wires and brooch pins—are obvious. But you can also incorporate all kinds of domestic hardware, from nuts and bolts to keys and drawer pulls, into your designs. Above all, try to personalize your jewelry by adding elements that have real meaning for you or the recipient.

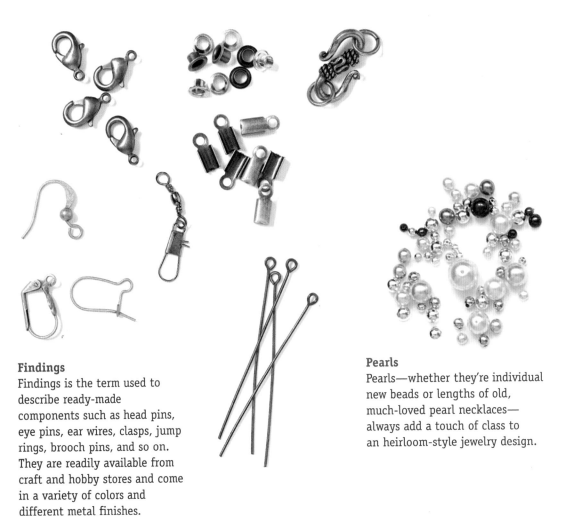

**Findings**
Findings is the term used to describe ready-made components such as head pins, eye pins, ear wires, clasps, jump rings, brooch pins, and so on. They are readily available from craft and hobby stores and come in a variety of colors and different metal finishes.

**Pearls**
Pearls—whether they're individual new beads or lengths of old, much-loved pearl necklaces—always add a touch of class to an heirloom-style jewelry design.

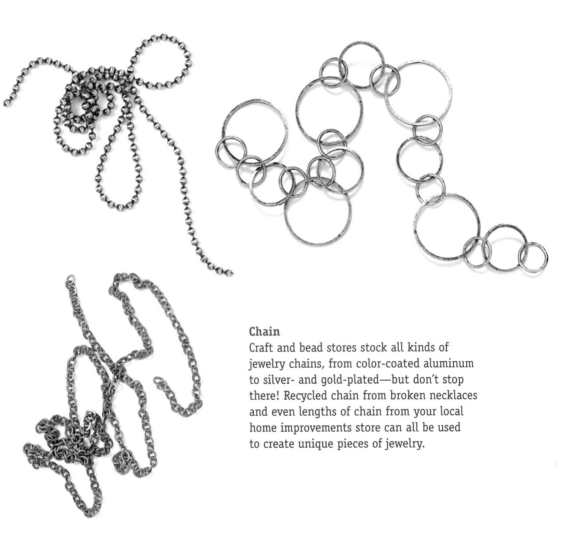

## Chain

Craft and bead stores stock all kinds of jewelry chains, from color-coated aluminum to silver- and gold-plated—but don't stop there! Recycled chain from broken necklaces and even lengths of chain from your local home improvements store can all be used to create unique pieces of jewelry.

## Buttons

Buttons can add weight, splashes of color, and a sense of fun to your jewelry. Unpick them from worn-out garments and save them in a button jar (a great decoration in its own right) until you decide what to do with them!

## Found objects

Dig out old keys, bottle caps, keyhole covers, and much more from their hiding places. As long as they're not too heavy or too big, they can easily be incorporated into necklaces and bracelets to add a funky, contemporary feel. Craft and scrapbooking stores now offer a large variety of reproduction "found objects" such as keys, brass tags, and miniature brass frames, all of which work well in jewelry, too.

## Recycled beads

Collect striking beads from old, broken jewelry pieces and use them as the starting point for a brand new design. You can also use centerpieces from brooches or vintage earrings and just snip off the findings from the back (see page 17).

## Bead sizes

This illustration shows the actual size of beads up to 12mm, along with a handy ruler that you can use to measure beads when you go shopping.

1mm    2mm    3mm    4mm    5mm    6mm

7mm    8mm    9mm    10mm    11mm    12mm

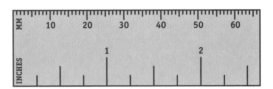

# Techniques

A few simple techniques are all you need to start making your own jewelry. Follow the instructions below and you'll be creating stylish, one-of-a-kind pieces in next to no time!

## Opening and closing jump rings

Jump rings are used to link different elements of your design together. You can buy them ready made, in a range of different sizes.

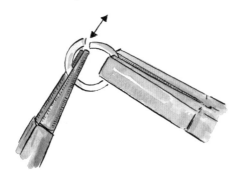

Grasp the jump ring with pliers on each side of the slit, then gently push one side of the ring away from the other. Do not attempt to open a jump ring by pulling the ends apart, because this will distort the shape and it will be hard to get it back into a perfect circle. When you have added your charm or bead, close the jump ring by repeating the pushing action in reverse.

## Forming a loop

When you thread beads onto a head pin, you need to form the other end of the pin into a loop, so that you can attach the bead to your necklace chain or ear wire.

**1** Thread the bead onto the head pin, then cut off the excess wire about ⅜ in. (1 cm) above the bead. Holding the wire vertically, use your round-nose pliers to bend the wire at a right angle.

**2** Hold the cut end of the wire tightly in your round-nose pliers and curl it round to form a loop, following the contour of your pliers.

## Making a wrapped loop

Wrapped loops are a great, secure way to create a closed loop without the use of solder or to create a closed loop that needs to be an irregular shape.

**1** Thread your bead onto a head pin or eye pin. Using flat- or chain-nose pliers, bend the wire above the bead at a right angle.

**2** Hold the wire at the bend in your round-nose pliers. Using chain-nose pliers, bring the wire around to form a loop, then wrap the wire around the stem several times until it touches the bead. Cut off any excess wire, then press the cut end firmly with flat-nose pliers so that it doesn't stick out.

## Using crimp covers

Crimp covers are a great way to cover up both crimp beads and ugly wraps of wire. You can attach them using either special crimp pliers or your everyday flat-nose pliers.

**1** Crimp covers are like little beads that are open on one side. Simply slip the cover over the wire(s) that you want to hide. (If necessary, use chain-nose pliers to gently prise the cover open wide enough.)

**2** Using either flat-nose pliers or crimp pliers, gently squeeze the sides of the crimp cover until they close tightly around the wires.

# Drilling holes in metal and enamel

Several of the projects in this book require you to drill holes in pieces of jewelry so that you can connect them together. You will need a marker pen, a wooden block, a center punch, a drill or dremel tool, and a drill bit of the appropriate size.

**2** Place the piece on a wooden block. Fit your drill with a bit of the appropriate size. Making sure the bit is vertical, carefully drill through the piece until the hole is complete.

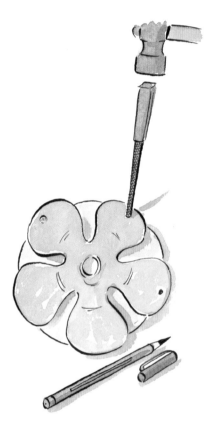

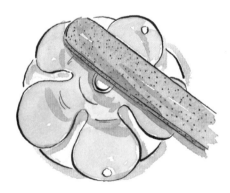

**1** Using a permanent marker pen, mark where you want the hole to be. Position the tip of a center punch over your mark, then strike the punch gently with a hammer to make a small indentation; this will help stop the drill bit from slipping.

**3** Turn the piece over and file down any rough edges around the hole.

## Snipping off findings

When I incorporate vintage jewelry into my designs, I often find that the original findings (pins, clasps, earring posts, and so on) are no longer required. I need to get rid of them in order for the piece to sit flat in the new design.

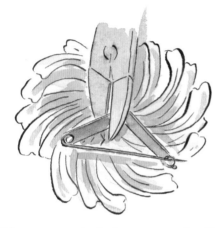

**1** Using your standard wire cutters, snip off the finding as close to the base as possible.

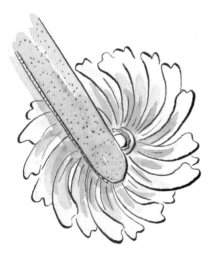

**2** File the base of the original finding until it is smooth.

## Applying patina solution

Patina solution such as black max is used to give an aged look to metals or to highlight the raised edges of stamped or embossed pieces. There are many different types of patina solutions available. It is a good idea to test a small area first, making sure that you follow the manufacturer's instructions.

**1** Using a cotton bud, apply patina solution to the piece of jewelry until you get the shade you want; it usually takes around 30 seconds.

**2** Rub a scouring pad across any raised areas; this will remove some of the surface patina to create a highlight. Rinse in clear water, dry, then polish with a polishing cloth.

# Chapter 1

# Vintage Finds

Vintage finds are found objects that you
may have in your house, find at an
antiques fair, or have been collecting for
many years. In this chapter you will be
able to use your treasures to assemble new
designs and show them off.

# Spring Iris Necklace

Enameled flowers blossomed in the 1960s, creating a colorful radiance of blooms to adorn garments. Due to large-scale production, vintage pins such as the one I've used here are widely available and easy to find.

## Materials

Enamel pin (brooch)

5 x 8mm jump rings

2 x 12-in. (30-cm) lengths of vintage chain

Lobster clasp

## Tools

Chain-, flat-, and round-nose pliers

Wire cutters

**1** If the finding on the back of your pin (brooch) runs horizontally rather than vertically, use chain-nose pliers to turn it around. Using wire cutters, cut off the pin below the central rivet, as close to the rivet as possible. Then cut off the pin above the rivet, leaving about ⅜ in. (1 cm) protruding.

**2** Using round-nose pliers, curl the ⅜-in. (1-cm) end of the pin into a loop.

**3** Attach an 8mm jump ring to the loop you have just made (see page 14). Use two more jump rings to attach two lengths of chain to the jump ring above the loop.

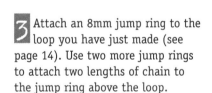

**4** Attach a jump ring to the end of the right-hand chain and a jump ring and lobster clasp to the end of the left-hand chain.

# Teal Cameo Necklace

The cameo is an accessory that has survived the whims of changing fashion. Queen Victoria and Catherine the Great were among the many who adorned themselves with cameos. This design is incredibly versatile, so choose your own jewels to showcase.

## Materials

Double-standed necklace

3 large jump rings

Cameo pendant

## Tools

Chain-nose pliers

Flat-nose pliers

1 Lay the double-stranded necklace vertically in front of you, with the clasp at the top and the small beaded chain (into which the clasp is linked to close the necklace) at the bottom.

2 Decide how long a drop you want for the pendant and, if necessary, remove any surplus links from the small beaded chain. Open a jump ring, thread it through the hanging loop of the cameo pendant and the last link of the small-beaded chain, then close the jump ring (see page 14).

☞ This concept works well with many double-stranded necklaces. If there is a significant difference in length between the two strands, just add some chain to the shorter side.

3 Remove the strand connector from the clasp end of the necklace by gently opening the knot cover, then close the knot cover again. (These are delicate: if you break the closure, simply glue a new one on top of the existing one!)

**4** Remove the fish-hook clasp from the strand connector that you have just taken off your necklace and attach it to the knot cover of the shortest side of the string of beads via a jump ring.

**5** Attach a jump ring to the knot cover of the longest side of the string of beads.

# Simplicity Earrings

This understated design makes a style statement. I love the elegance of chandeliers in grandiose settings illuminating the beauty in a room; these sparkling crystal earrings will allow your own beauty to shine.

**Materials**

2 x 3½ in. (9-cm) wire pins

2 x 12mm rondelle beads with Swarovski crystals

2 chandelier crystal drops, approx. 1½ in. (4 cm) long

2 crimp bead covers

2 ear wires

**Tools**

Beading mat

Chain-, flat-, and round-nose pliers

Wire cutters

**1** Using round-nose pliers, form a small wrapped loop (see page 15) at one end of the wire pin.

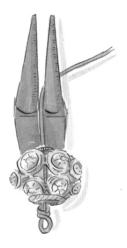

**2** Thread one rondelle bead onto the open end of the wire pin and push it up against the loop. Starting ⅜ in. (1 cm) from the base of the crystal bead, using the widest part of your round-nose pliers, make the beginning of a large wrapped loop. Thread a chandelier crystal drop onto the wire pin and complete the wrapped loop. Cut off any excess pin wire.

 Swarovski elements add glint to any piece that lacks pizzazz! They are easy to find at your local craft stores and are available in a large variety. Using long head pins allows you to adjust the finished length.

**3** Cover the wrapped wire below the rondelle bead with a crimp bead cover (see page 15).

**4** Open the loop at the base of the ear wire, hook it over the small wrapped loop above the Swarovski bead, and close again. Repeat steps 1–4 to make the second earring.

**Note:** Be sure to pay attention to the weight of the crystals you are buying—some are heavier than they look!

*"Simplicity is the ultimate sophistication."*

Leonardo da Vinci

# Triple-Strand Necklace

By marrying two upper-class elements together, this debutante design makes its way back into society. With the formal affairs of yesterday and the affairs of today you can mix any two elements to the center strand to accentuate your event. Triple-strand necklaces are still readily available and easy to use.

## Materials

Triple-strand vintage necklace

2 lengths of chain (see no

Brooch, at least 1½ in. (4 cm) in diameter

4 x 7mm jump rings

## Tools

Beading mat

Chain- and flat-nose plier

Wire cutters

File

**1** Lay the triple-strand necklace horizontally in front of you, with the fastener on right and the linked beaded chain on the left. Using chain-nose pliers, remove the center strand of beads from the necklace.

**2** Using wire cutters, cut off the pin bar from the back of the brooch, cutting as close to the base as possible. File down any rough ridges and wipe clean (see page 17).

**3** Using a jump ring, attach one end of a length of chain to the center hole of the left-hand 4-ringed strand connector. Repeat on the right-hand side, using the other length of chain.

**4** Using jump rings, attach the brooch between the two free ends of the chains.

☞ The amount of chain that you need depends on the length of your necklace. Measure the center strand of your triple-strand necklace; you will need the same length of chain, minus the diameter of your brooch, cut into two equal lengths.

# Flower Garden Necklace

With large, bold enamel designs, as here, you can create your own everlasting garden of flowering blooms.

## Materials

3 large enamel pins

10mm jump rings

Earring (optional)

6 x 8-in. (20-cm) beaded chains

Lobster clasp

## Tools

Beading mat

Wire cutters

File

Marker pen

Wooden block

Center punch

Drill and $^1/_{16}$-in. (1.5-mm) drill bit

Chain- and flat-nose pliers

Jewelry glue

Toothpick

**1** Lay the enamel pins horizontally on your beading mat in your chosen order.

**2** If necessary, use wire cutters to snip off the pin findings, file down any rough ridges, and wipe clean (see page 17).

**3** You now need to drill holes in the pins, so that you can connect them together. Work out where the holes need to go: you will need one at the top of the left-hand piece and one at the top of the right-hand piece for the chains, plus holes to connect the three pins together. Mark the hole positions with a marker pen. Lay one piece at a time on your wooden block, right side down, make a small indentation with a center punch at the marked spots, and then drill a $^1/_{16}$-in. (1.5-mm) hole in each one.

☞ When drilling holes, do not let go of the piece and make sure you hold it securely. On some enamel, you may get chipping; this can be prevented (or at least minimized) if you drill from the back of the piece.

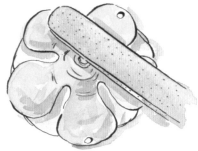

**4** File the edges of the holes on the backs of the pins to smooth the edges.

**5** Put all the pieces back on your beading mat in the right order and connect them together using jump rings (see page 14).

**6** The center of the largest flower in my design was a flat enamel button; I wanted to make it more three-dimensional, so I replaced it with a vintage clip earring, from which I cut off the clip fastening (see page 17); I then glued it in place with jewelry glue and left it to dry.

**7** Take three 8-in. (20-cm) lengths of beaded chain, open a 10mm jump ring, loop it through the last link of all three chains and the right-hand hole you drilled for chains in step 3, then close the jump ring again. Repeat on the left-hand side of the necklace with the remaining three chains.

**8** Attach a large jump ring to the last link of the three chains on the right-hand side of the necklace. Attach a large jump ring and a lobster clasp to the last link of the three chains on the left-hand side of the necklace.

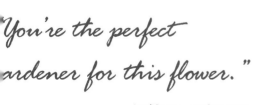

*"You're the perfect gardener for this flower."*

Author unknown

# Layered Stranded Necklace

This design is simple in nature but has a luxurious and lavish look.

## Materials

3 triple-strand vintage necklaces

13 x 7mm jump rings

1 x 10-19-in. (25-48-cm) length of chain

Center pendant of your choice: I made mine from a bronze bird, a large pearl bead, and a vintage earring

## Tools

Beading mat

Chain- and flat-nose pliers

**1** Lay the three triple-strand necklaces horizontally in front of you, with the closure end on the left, in order of length—the shortest necklace (#1) at the top, the medium-length necklace (#2) in the center, and the longest necklace (#3) at the bottom.

**2** Using your chain- and flat-nose pliers, remove the center and bottom strands from necklace #1, the center strand of necklace #2, and all three strands of necklace #3.

**3** Using jump rings, attach the strands you removed from necklaces #2 and #3 to the strand connectors of necklace #1: attach the strand from necklace #2 to the center holes and all three strands of necklace #3 to the bottom holes.

☞ If you attach a lobster clasp to each end of your pendant strand, you can remove it from the multi-strand necklace and use it as a single-strand necklace as well.

**4** Measure the chain to which you're going to attach your pendant and embellishments against the length of your necklaces and decide how long you want it to be. Cut to length if necessary.

**5** Design your center pendant: I attached a pearl connector bead to the base of a bronze bird pendant, and a vintage earring to the base of the connector bead. Then attach the pendant to the center of the chain.

**6** Using jump rings, attach the pendant chain to the center holes of the strand connector of necklace 1.

# Bejeweled Ribbon Bracelet

With its soft texture and elegant sheen, silk fabric adds a luxurious touch to any craft project. Here it is torn into strips to give an edgy, contemporary feel.

## Materials

Enamel brooch, 2 in. (5 cm) in diameter

6 x 6-in. (15-cm) strands of dyed silk, approx. 1 in. (2.5 cm) wide

6 fold-over crimps

8 x 7mm split rings

2 x 4-ringed strand connectors

Lobster clasp

6 x 4-in. (10-cm) strands of dyed silk, approx. 1 in. (2.5 cm) wide

## Tools

Wire cutters

File

Marker pen

Wooden block

Center punch

Drill and ⁵⁄₃₂-in. (4-mm) drill bit

Beading mat

Chain- and flat-nose pliers

Jewelry glue

Toothpick

Scissors

1 Using wire cutters, cut the pin off the back of the brooch as close to the pin base as possible. File down any rough ridges and wipe clean (see page 17).

2 My brooch had gaps around the edge into which I could tie the silk strands. If yours does not, mark three evenly spaced holes on each side of the brooch. Lay the brooch on a wooden block, make a small indentation with a center punch, and drill a ⁵⁄₃₂-in. (4-mm) hole at each marked point. Then turn the brooch over and file the area around the holes to smooth the edges (see page 16).

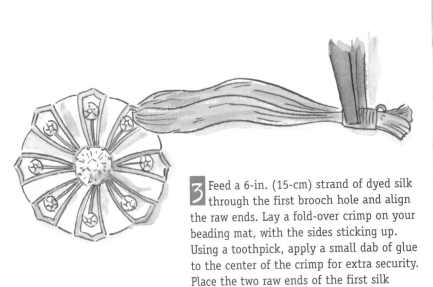

3 Feed a 6-in. (15-cm) strand of dyed silk through the first brooch hole and align the raw ends. Lay a fold-over crimp on your beading mat, with the sides sticking up. Using a toothpick, apply a small dab of glue to the center of the crimp for extra security. Place the two raw ends of the first silk strand in the crimp. Using your flat-nose pliers, fold the sides of the crimp up and crimp as tightly as you can. Repeat until you have attached three strands of silk to each side of the brooch.

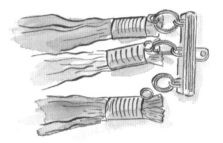

4 Using split rings, connect each crimp to the appropriate hole in a 4-ringed strand connector.

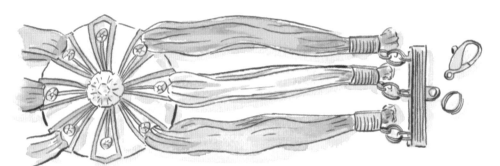

5 Attach a split ring to the top loop of the right-hand 4-ringed strand connector and a split ring and lobster clasp to the top loop of the left-hand 4-ringed strand connector.

**6** Tie one 4-in. (10-cm) strand of dyed silk over each fold-over crimp on the front of the bracelet and trim the ends.

☞ Choose colors of silk that blend in with the colors in your chosen centerpiece. If you prefer a neater, more "finished" look, use wide silk ribbon instead of tearing fabric into strips.

# Chapter 2

# Charmed

From childhood to adulthood, designs that
use trinkets and charms never lose their
appeal. This chapter is packed with ideas
for creating pieces of jewelry that each
have their own individual story to tell.

# Sweet Sentiments Necklace

All kinds of objects can trigger memories and associations: a hotel key tag can remind us of a romantic weekend, a fragment of broken jewelry of a special friend, a button of a favorite dress... Collect your own charms and create a memory necklace of sweet sentiments.

 Arrange your chosen charms in order on your beading mat.

### Materials

5 charms of your choice: I used an optical lens, an embellished key, an embellished watch face, a large crystal drop, and a hotel key tag

5 jump rings

16-in. (40-cm) large-linked chain

2 x 7mm split rings

Lobster clasp

### Tools

Beading mat

Chain- and flat-nose pliers

2 Find the center link of the chain. Using a jump ring, attach your center charm (I used an embellished watch face) to this link (see page 14).

3 Add the remaining charms at four-link intervals in the same way—two to the right of the center charm and two to the left.

Large-linked chain works best for this design. When creating this piece look for treasures that are similar in size; if you want a fuller look, find smaller treasures to attach between the larger ones.

**4** Attach a split ring to the right-hand end of the chain and a split ring and a lobster clasp to the left-hand end.

# Class Act Bracelet

You can make almost any design with brass tags. Their shape and gentle flexibility help make the design process easier and versatile. Aside from having something unique, you're putting industrial tags into a class of their own.

## Materials

Locker tag 2¾ in. (7 cm) long

Approx. 4½ in. (12 cm) large-linked chain

1 x 7mm jump ring

Lobster clasp

2 x 2-in. (5-cm) head pins

1 x 6mm pearl bead

1 x 6mm crystal bead

1 x shank button, approx. ½ in. (14 mm) in diameter

1 x 10mm jump ring

## Tools

Beading mat

Chain-, flat-, and round-nose pliers

Wire cutters

Rolling pin or cup

**1** Bend the tag around a curved object such as a cup or rolling pin by applying gentle pressure.

**2** Cut your chain to the length you need to complete the bracelet: a standard bracelet is 7¼ in. (18.5 cm) long and the tag shown here is 2¾ in. (7 cm) long, so I cut my chain to 4½ in. (12 cm)—but it all depends on the size of your tag.

**3** Open the end link of the chain, loop it through the hole in the left-hand side of the tag, then close the link again (see page 14).

This bracelet looks great with several lengths of chain linked together. Add your favorite items as charms—the sky's the limit!

4 Loop a jump ring through the link on the lobster clasp and the last link of the other end of the chain.

5 Open a left-over chain link, loop it through the hole on the right-hand side of the tag, then close the chain link again; you will connect the lobster clasp to this to close the bracelet.

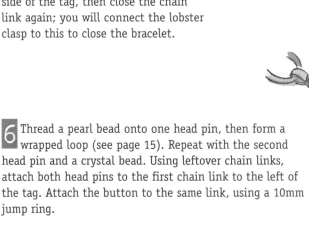

6 Thread a pearl bead onto one head pin, then form a wrapped loop (see page 15). Repeat with the second head pin and a crystal bead. Using leftover chain links, attach both head pins to the first chain link to the left of the tag. Attach the button to the same link, using a 10mm jump ring.

# Decanter Tag Necklace

Since the early 1700s, silversmiths have designed and created decanter tags to identify and add beauty to the ordinary necks of bottles. If you can't find a vintage tag that you like, reproduction versions are readily available.

## Materials

Decanter tag

2 x 8-in. (20-cm) lengths of chain

5 x 5mm jump rings

Lobster clasp

1 x 2-in. (5-cm) head pin

3–4 embellishments: I used an opaque white glass bead, a flower charm, and a pearl button with shank

## Tools

Beading mat

Chain-, flat-, and round-nose pliers

Wire cutters

1 Remove the existing chain from the decanter tag, leaving the jump rings attached to the tag. Attach one 8-in. (20-cm) chain length to each side of the tag.

2 Using 5mm jump rings, attach a jump ring to the end of the right-hand chain and a jump ring and a lobster clasp to the end of the left-hand chain (see page 14).

☞ Take your initials or family name, print on an adhesive paper and create a decanter label of your own by using a Mod Podge or decoupage technique.

3 Thread the opaque white glass bead onto a 2-in. (5-cm) head pin, pushing it right up to the end. Using your round-nose pliers, form a wrapped loop with the rest of the head pin (see page 15).

4 Using jump rings, attach the opaque white glass bead and your other embellishments to the jump ring to the left of the tag (see page 14).

# Victor Tag Necklace

Nothing evokes the past as effectively as music. This tag, which features the Victor Talking Machine Company's famous trademark of the fox terrier Nipper listening to a wind-up gramophone, is sure to bring back memories of the music that filled our grandparents' and great-grandparents' homes.

## Materials

Victor Talking Machine Co. tag (or tag of your choice)

2 x 8-in. (20-cm) lengths of blue linked chain

7 x 7mm jump rings

1 x 8-in. (20-cm) length of pearl linked chain

1 x 17-in. (43-cm) length of pink linked chain

1 x 14-in. (35-cm) length of bronze snake chain

Lobster clasp

3-in. (7.5-cm) wire pin

Crystal teardrop pendant, 1¼ in. (3 cm) long

1 x 10mm crimp cover bead

## Tools

Beading mat

Chain-, flat-, and round-nose pliers

Wire cutters

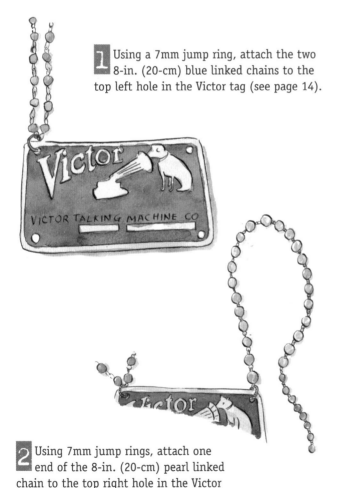

**1** Using a 7mm jump ring, attach the two 8-in. (20-cm) blue linked chains to the top left hole in the Victor tag (see page 14).

**2** Using 7mm jump rings, attach one end of the 8-in. (20-cm) pearl linked chain to the top right hole in the Victor tag and the other end to one end of the 17-in. (34-cm) pink linked chain.

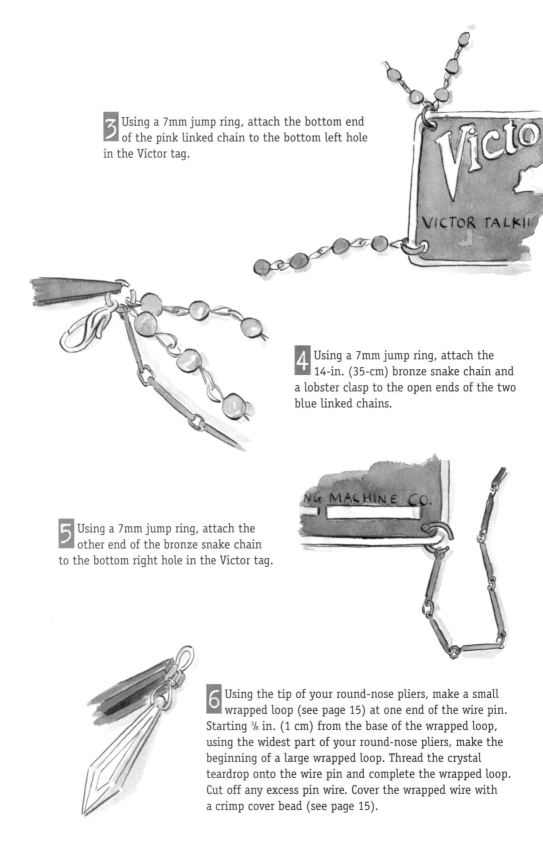

**3** Using a 7mm jump ring, attach the bottom end of the pink linked chain to the bottom left hole in the Victor tag.

**4** Using a 7mm jump ring, attach the 14-in. (35-cm) bronze snake chain and a lobster clasp to the open ends of the two blue linked chains.

**5** Using a 7mm jump ring, attach the other end of the bronze snake chain to the bottom right hole in the Victor tag.

**6** Using the tip of your round-nose pliers, make a small wrapped loop (see page 15) at one end of the wire pin. Starting ³/₈ in. (1 cm) from the base of the wrapped loop, using the widest part of your round-nose pliers, make the beginning of a large wrapped loop. Thread the crystal teardrop onto the wire pin and complete the wrapped loop. Cut off any excess pin wire. Cover the wrapped wire with a crimp cover bead (see page 15).

**7** Using a 7mm jump ring, attach the crystal teardrop pendant to the bottom right hole in the Victor tag.

☞ Online auctions and flea markets are great sources of tags. If you find a tag that you really like and it doesn't have holes, make them using a metal punch, a drill with a small drill bit, or a hammer and nail.

# Charm Earrings

In these earrings, many tiny symbolic
charms are assembled together to create
a big, bold statement.

## Materials

2 x 15mm pearl buttons with
  shanks

2 x 2-in. (5-cm) eye pins

Jump rings

2 ear wires

1 small spacer bead

2 x pink and silver
  rhinestone spacer beads

2 x 6mm Swarovski crystals

1 x 8mm pearl bead

Large jump ring

1 lightweight pewter cross

1 lightweight copper cross

1 lightweight small brass
  locket

1 rhinestone vintage charm

2 x 2-in. (5-cm) head pins

Scraps of chain

## Tools

Wire cutters

Chain-, flat-, and round-nose
  pliers

**1** Thread the shank of a pearl button
onto an eye pin, then cut the stem
of the pin ⅜ in. (1 cm) above the button.
Using round-nose pliers, begin curling
the stem into a loop, add a jump ring,
then complete the loop.

**2** Half open the original head
pin loop, attach an ear wire,
and close. Repeat steps 1 and 2
for the second earring.

**3** Thread a small spacer bead, a pink-and-silver rhinestone
spacer bead, and a 6mm Swarovski crystal bead onto a head
pin and form a wrapped loop (see page 15). Using a jump ring,
attach the crystal and rhinestone combination to the bottom of
a 1-in. (2.5-cm) length of scrap chain, then use another jump
ring to attach the top of the chain to the jump ring of a pearl
button. Thread a 6mm Swarovski crystal bead, a pink-and-silver
rhinestone spacer bead, and the 8mm pearl bead onto the
other head pin and form a wrapped loop. Attach to the jump
ring of the other pearl button with the large jump ring.

**4** Using jump rings, attach the pewter cross to the jump ring of one pearl button and the copper cross to the jump ring of the other pearl button.

**5** Attach the top of a ¾-in. (2-cm) length of beaded chain to the jump ring of the pearl button with the pewter cross. Using round-nose pliers, open the bottom link of the beaded chain, attach a small brass locket, then close the link.

**6** Attach the top of a 1¼-in. (3-cm) length of beaded chain to the jump ring of the pearl button with the copper cross. Using round-nose pliers, open the bottom link of the beaded chain, attach a small rhinestone charm, then close the link.

# Multi-Tag Necklace

These vintage metal number tags were once used to define one's assigned personal space on lockers, gym baskets, mailboxes, and doors. Find number tags that have a special meaning for you—perhaps your date of birth, or a special anniversary—and incorporate them into a piece of jewelry that is unique to you.

## Materials

7 brass tags

Brass pin

7 x 9–12mm jump rings or chain links

Typewriter key

2 x 2-in. (5-cm) chains

Lobster clasp

## Tools

Beading mat

Wire cutters

File

Marker pen

Wooden block

Center punch

Drill and $^1/_{16}$-in. (1.5-mm) drill bit

Chain- and flat-nose pliers

Jewelry glue

Toothpick to apply glue

1 Lay the brass tags and pin on a beading mat, with the pin at the center, in your chosen order.

2 If necessary, use wire cutters to snip off any posts or findings from the back of your tags and pin, file down any rough ridges, and wipe clean (see page 17).

3 Decide where you need to make holes on the brass pin so that you can attach the other elements to it. (I used three holes on this design.) Lay the pin on a wooden block, make a small indentation with a center punch at the marked spots, and then drill $^1/_{16}$-in. (1.5-mm) holes at the marked points.

**4** Turn the pin over and file the area around the holes to smooth the edges (see page 16).

**5** Lay all the pieces back on the beading mat in the correct order. Using a jump ring or chain link, attach the first tag to the bottom of the brass pin (see page 14).

**6** Attach the six remaining tags in the same way—three on each side of the brass pin.

**7** Apply a dab of jewelry glue to the center of the brass pin and attach the typewriter key. Leave to dry.

**8** Using chain links or jump rings, attach one 2-in. (5-cm) chain length to each side of the necklace. Attach a jump ring to the end of the right-hand chain and a jump ring and a lobster clasp to the end of the left-hand chain.

"An artist is not paid for his labor, but for his vision."

James McNeill Whistler

# Trinkets Bracelet

Charms are symbols that remind us of where we have been and where we may yet go. Collect your own charms for a unique piece of jewelry that reflects your life—past, present, and future.

## Materials

7-in. (18-cm) gold large-linked chain

22 large chain links

Lobster clasp

7 pearl buttons with shanks

13 charms of your choice: my charms included a tintype, drawer pull, brass tag, pearl buttons, and a crystal drop

## Tools

Beading mat

Chain- and flat-nose pliers

1 Place the gold large-linked chain horizontally in front of you on the beading mat. Using chain-nose pliers, attach a large chain link to the last link on the right-hand side of chain and a large chain link and a lobster clasp to the last link on the left-hand side of the chain.

2 Now lay the chain vertically, with the clasp at the top. Using a large chain link and looping it through the shank of a pearl button, attach a button to the first link of the chain below the clasp. Repeat down the right-hand side of the bracelet, spacing the buttons evenly, until you have used up all seven buttons.

☞ Using charms that are similar in color or from the same era will help make the design look more cohesive.

3 Arrange the charms on your beading mat in your order of choice. (Try to alternate large and small, to create a balanced design.) Flip the gold chain from right to left, so that the buttons are now on the left-hand side. Using large chain links, attach your charms in your desired order.

# Chapter 3

# Hardware

Hardware—keys, keyhole covers, even drawer pulls—are not generally thought of as things that belong in the world of designer jewelry and are often discarded when no longer required for their original purpose. This chapter shows how you can recycle, repurpose, and revise both old and new hardware into beautiful creations.

# Gate Keeper Earrings

Whether they're for our car, home, or a box of treasured memories, keys are part of our everyday lives. What might the keys in this design unlock?

1 Clean the keys if necessary and lay them flat in front of you on a beading mat. Using a toothpick, apply a small dab of jewelry glue to the center of each key and attach a 5mm flat-backed crystal to each one. Leave to dry.

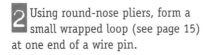

2 Using round-nose pliers, form a small wrapped loop (see page 15) at one end of a wire pin.

## Materials

2 flat lightweight keys

2 x 5mm flat-backed crystals

2 x 3½-in. (9-cm) wire pins

2 x 6mm crystal beads

2 crimp bead covers

2 ear wires

## Tools

Beading mat

Toothpick

Jewelry glue

Chain-, flat-, and round-nose pliers

Wire cutters

✿ VARIATION: Why not use fabric flowers or small treasures instead of beads with these key earrings?

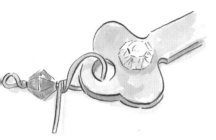

3 Thread a 6mm crystal bead onto the open end of the eye pin and push it up against the loop. Starting ⅜ in. (1 cm) from the base of the crystal bead, using the widest part of your round-nose pliers, make the beginning of a large wrapped loop. Thread the key onto the pin and complete the wrapped loop. Cut off any excess pin wire.

4 Cover the wrapped wire below the crystal bead with a crimp bead cover (see page 15).

5 Open the loop at the base of the ear wire, hook it over the small wrapped loop above the crystal bead, and close again. Repeat steps 2–5 for the second earring.

# Keyhole & Crystal Necklace

This necklace combines an industrial-looking keyhole cover with a large, elegant, sparkling crystal drop, creating a design that is both bold and delicate. The multiple strands of chain balance the design.

## Materials

24 in. (60 cm) each of three strands of chain

4 x 12mm jump rings

Lobster clasp

Keyhole cover, approx. 1¾ x 1 in. (4.5 x 2.5 cm)

Crystal drop, approx. 2 in. (5 cm) long

## Tools

Beading mat

Chain-nose pliers

Flat-nose pliers

**1** Lay the three strands of chain horizontally in front of you on the beading mat.

**2** Open a 12mm jump ring, feed it through last link of the three chains on the right-hand side of the mat, and close the jump ring (see page 14). Open another 12mm jump ring, feed it through last link of the three chains on the left-hand side, add the lobster clasp, and close.

*"A very little key will open a very heavy door."*

Charles Dickens

**3** Open a 12mm jump ring, thread it through the screw hole at the top of the keyhole cover, lay the three lengths of chain in the jump ring, and close the jump ring.

**4** Open the last 12mm jump ring, thread it through the screw hole in the bottom of the keyhole cover and the top of the crystal drop, then close the jump ring.

☞ Paint your keyhole cover any color you wish and scruff it up with sandpaper to age it. Find a treasure and add it to the bottom of the keyhole.

# Rococo Necklace

Drawer pulls have been around for centuries, but the beauty of their flowing Rococo curves is often overlooked. By taking them off the large pieces they once adorned and adding feminine frills to soften their appearance, you can create a striking piece of jewelry with a style of its very own.

**Materials**

Decorative drawer pull plate

2 x 8-in. (20-cm) lengths of chain

2 x 12mm chain links

3 x 6mm jump rings

Lobster clasp

Vintage earring for center embellishment

14mm octagonal crystal

8mm pink flower charm

**Tools**

Beading mat

Chain- and flat-nose pliers

Wire cutters

File

Jewelry glue

Toothpick

1 Using 12mm chain links, attach one length of chain to each side of the drawer pull plate (see page 14).

2 Attach a 6mm jump ring to the end of the right-hand chain and a 6mm jump ring and a lobster clasp to the end of the left-hand chain.

Inexpensive domestic hardware is great to use in jewelry designs: just keep an eye out for the hole placements. You can use this design with most styles and enhance the design of the hardware through your choice of embellishments. Mix and match old and new!

3 If necessary, use wire cutters to snip off any post or finding from the back of the vintage earring, file smooth, and wipe clean (see page 17). Using a toothpick, apply a dab of jewelry glue to the center of the drawer pull plate and stick the vintage earring in place. Leave to dry.

4 Using a 6mm jump ring, attach the pink flower charm to the bottom loop on the octagonal crystal. Open the top loop on the crystal with your round-nose pliers, then attach the crystal to one side of the chain, 3 in. (7.5 cm) above the drawer pull plate.

# Impressions Necklace

One definition of the word "impression" is "a telling image impressed on the senses or the mind." With this necklace, stamped with a special word or phrase, you get to choose the impression that you make!

## Materials

Flat key

Vintage-style earring

12mm jump ring

Ball chain necklace

## Tools

Beading mat

Steel block and hammer

Metal letter stamps

Cotton bud

Patina solution

Heavy-duty scouring pad

Flat- and chain-nose pliers

Wire cutters

File

Jewelry glue

Toothpick

**1** Lay the key flat on a steel block. Holding each letter stamp vertically on the key, tap the top with the hammer to stamp your chosen word letter by letter.

**2** Using a cotton bud, apply patina solution (see page 17) to the stamped side of the key in vertical strokes until you get the shade you want. Using a heavy-duty scouring pad, scrub the surface patina from the key until only the letters remain blackened. Rinse with water. Dry the key.

**3** If necessary, use wire cutters to snip off any post or finding from the back of your earring, file smooth, and wipe clean (see page 17).

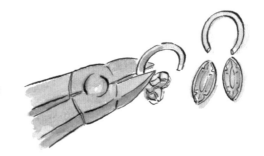

4 Using a toothpick, apply an appropriate amount of jewelry glue to the head of the key and set the earring in place. Leave to dry.

☞ This is a great use for those single earrings that gather at the bottom of your jewelry box and are hard to throw away, even when the other one of the pair has been lost. If possible, find embellishments that have a flat back for this design.

5 Open the 12mm jump ring, loop it through the top of the key, and close (see page 14). Thread the ball chain necklace through the jump ring.

# Quotations Key Necklace

Sometimes, we carry a saying or a quotation with us to get us through a particular period in our life. Use a quote that means something special to you in this piece or spell out the names of your children or loved ones.

## Materials

Flat keys—one for each word of your chosen phrase

Vintage bird pin

2 x 10-in. (25-cm) pearl linked chains

Pearl-and-bead linked necklace

Large lobster clasp

Large jump ring

14–20 x 7mm Swarovski crystals

## Tools

Beading mat

Steel block and hammer

Metal letter stamps

Patina solution

Cotton bud

Heavy-duty scouring pad

Round-, chain-, and flat-nose pliers

Wire cutters

Jewelry glue

Toothpick

1 Lay the first key flat on a steel block. Holding each metal stamp vertically, tap the top with the hammer to stamp the first word of your phrase letter by letter.

2 Using a cotton bud, apply patina solution to the key until you get the shade you want (see page 17). Using a heavy-duty scouring pad, scrub the surface patina from the key until only the letters remain blackened. Rinse with water, then dry the key.

3 Repeat steps 1–2 with the remaining keys, using a different key for each word of your chosen phrase, then lay the keys out in order on a beading mat. My phrase read, "I feel like a tiny bird with a big song."

**4** If the finding on the back of your pin (brooch) runs horizontally rather than vertically, use chain-nose pliers to turn it around. Using wire cutters, cut off the pin below the central rivet, as close to the rivet as possible. Then cut off the pin above the rivet, leaving about ⅜ in. (1 cm) protruding.

**5** I recycled part of a broken pearl-and-bead linked necklace for my necklace center and the leftover pearl links to attach the keys. The exact length of the necklace center will depend on the number of keys in your phrase, as you need one link for each key plus another one for the vintage pin. Using jump rings, attach one 10-in. (25-cm) length of pearl linked chain to each side of the necklace center.

**6** Attach a large jump ring to the left-hand end of the chain and a large jump ring and a lobster clasp to the right-hand end of the chain.

☞ Use embellishments that complement your phrase and make it come alive. If you want your necklace center to look exactly like this one but can't find the right style of vintage necklace, make your own connectors using beads and eye pins.

**7** Cut the required number of pearl beads from the left-over section of the pearl-and-bead linked necklace; you need one for each key, plus one for the vintage pin. Each pearl bead will have a loop on each side. Using jump rings, attach each key to the bottom of a pearl bead, then attach the keys to the necklace center by opening the top loop of the pearl bead with your round-nose pliers (see page 14), making sure the stamped words are in the right order.

**8** Using a jump ring, attach the vintage bird pin to the next chain link after the end of your phrase.

**9** Lay the necklace on a beading mat, with all the keys flat. Using a toothpick, apply tiny dabs of jewelry glue to each key and glue on Swarovski crystals. Leave to dry.

# Pulled Together Necklace

Using whimsy, combined with the most common object found at home on cabinets and doors, pull this design together! Before throwing out old pieces of furniture, be sure to remove the drawer knobs or pulls for use in your jewelry projects.

## Materials

28-in. (72-cm) length of large-linked Rolo brass chain

Lobster clasp

2 jump rings

22-gauge (0.6-mm) gunmetal wire

20-gauge (0.8-mm) burgundy wire

7 drawer knobs

12 x 7mm Swarovski crystals

8 x 15mm large crystal rondelles

## Tools

Beading mat

Chain-, round-, and flat-nose pliers

Wire cutters

1 Attach a jump ring to the right-hand end of the Rolo chain and a jump ring and a lobster clasp to the left-hand end of chain (see page 14).

2 Cut twelve 3-in. (7.5-cm) and four 8-in. (20-cm) lengths of 22-gauge (0.6-mm) wire, and eight 3-in. (7.5-cm) and three 8-in. (20-cm) lengths of 20-gauge (0.8-mm) wire.

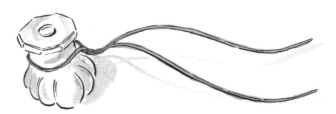

3 Lay the drawer knobs horizontally on your beading mat in your chosen order, starting with the largest piece toward the center. Wrap the center of an 8-in. (20-cm) length of wire around the neck of the first drawer knob and twist several times, so that it is tight and secure, leaving half the wire untwisted. Repeat with the remaining drawer knobs, alternating the colors of the wire.

4 Take a Swarovski crystal and thread it halfway down a 3-in. (7.5-cm) length of 22-gauge (0.6-mm) wire. Twist the two ends of the wire together to secure the crystal in place. Repeat with the remaining crystals.

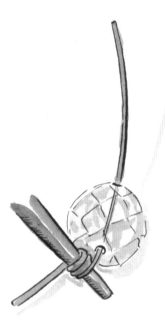

5 Curl one end of a 3-in. (7.5-cm) length of 20-gauge (0.8-mm) wire three times around the shaft of your round-nose pliers, then thread a large crystal rondelle onto the wire. Repeat with the remaining rondelles.

6 Find the center link of the Rolo chain and attach the first drawer knob by threading the excess wire through the chain link, folding it over, and twisting several times to secure.

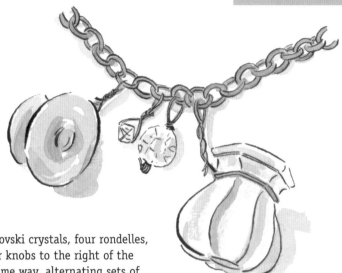

7 Attach five Swarovski crystals, four rondelles, and three drawer knobs to the right of the center link in the same way, alternating sets of two beads and a drawer knob and spacing them attractively. Repeat to the left of the center link.

☞ Have fun with this piece. Using wire allows you to add many embellishments that you may not be able to use with a basic jump ring.

8 To finish off your necklace, take your round-nose pliers and twist any loose ends of wire up tight against the chain.

# Time Ticking Necklace

It sometimes seems like our lives are governed by clocks and watches—we start to rush from the very moment we wake up. Wear this design to remind you to slow down and enjoy this beautiful life.

## Materials

Two 8-in. (20-cm) lengths of chain

Clock key approx. 2½ in. (6 cm) tall

4 x 5mm jump rings

Lobster clasp

1 center embellishment: I used an earring center

## Tools

Beading mat

Chain- and flat-nose pliers

Wire cutters

File

Toothpick

Jewelry glue

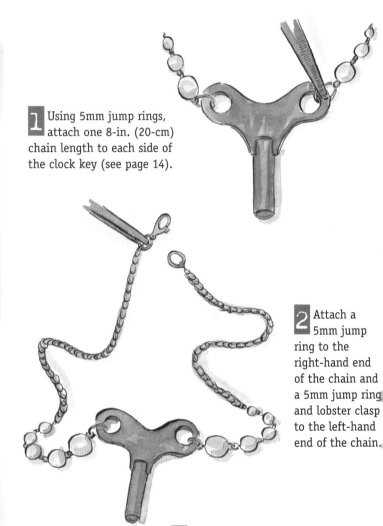

1 Using 5mm jump rings, attach one 8-in. (20-cm) chain length to each side of the clock key (see page 14).

2 Attach a 5mm jump ring to the right-hand end of the chain and a 5mm jump ring and lobster clasp to the left-hand end of the chain.

3 If necessary, use wire cutters to snip off any backing from your center embellishment, file down any rough ridges, and wipe clean (see page 17).

4 Clean the key if necessary and lay it flat in front of you on a beading mat. Using a toothpick, apply a dab of jewelry glue to the center of the key and attach the center embellishment. Leave to dry.

# Key Cuff

This soft leather cuff makes a daring statement on the wrist. Use your own sense of style to accentuate your cuff creation: whether you use intricate embroidery or flashy findings, you can make this fit any season or style.

## Materials

Strip of rust-colored leather, approx. 9½ x 2½ in. (24 x 6.5 cm)

Scrap of lace

2 buttons, approx. ½ in. (12 mm) and ¾ in. (20 mm) in diameter

Key

Scrap of silk

18-in. (45-cm) leather cord

## Tools

Beading mat

Needle

Quilting thread

Scissors

Chain-nose pliers

Steel block and hammer

Metal letter stamps

Patina solution

Cotton bud

Heavy-duty scouring pad

Toothpick

Jewelry glue

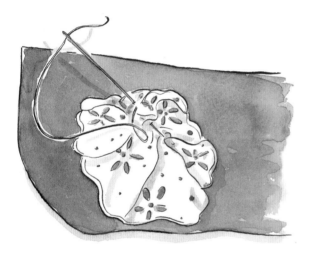

**1** Using a needle and quilting thread, which is stronger than ordinary sewing thread, begin stitching the scrap of lace onto the leather strip about 2 in. (5 cm) away from one short end, bunching the lace up slightly as you go. (Depending on how thick the leather is, you may need to use chain-nose pliers to help you pull the needle through.) Tie the thread in a knot on the back of the leather strip and trim off any excess.

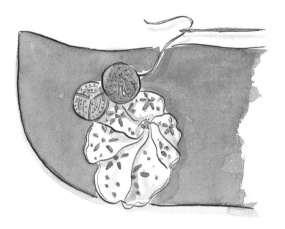

2 Again using quilting thread, sew the buttons onto same short end of the strip, so that you can wrap the leather around them when wearing the cuff to keep it on your wrist. Tie the threads in a knot on the back of the leather strip and trim off any excess.

3 Lay the key flat on a steel block. Holding each metal stamp vertically, tap the top with the hammer to stamp your chosen word letter by letter.

4 Using a cotton bud, apply patina solution to the key until you get the shade you want (see page 17).

5 Using a heavy-duty scouring pad, scrub the surface patina from the key until only the letters remain blackened. Rinse with water, then dry the key.

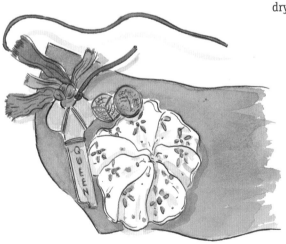

6 Sew the key to the leather wherever you feel it works best. (You may want to use a small amount of jewelry glue to help attach it to the leather.) Tie scraps of silk and the leather cord to the hole at the top of the key.

**7** Using a toothpick, apply a tiny amount of jewelry glue over the thread knots on the back of the leather strip for extra security. If you wish, glue another strip to the back of band so that the knots are not visible.

**8** Fasten the cuff by wrapping the leather cord around your wrist and then around the buttons.

 Simpler than some of the projects in this book, this is a great design for using up any odd scraps.

*"When one door closes, one will open."*

Sandra McCann

# Rosette Necklace

What I love about the centerpiece of this necklace is that although it is really a piece of hardware that originally adorned the wooden doors of old farmhouses, it has a beautiful name—a rosette. To give this salvaged item a design fit for its name, I used soft hues of pinks and delicate accents.

## Materials

2 x 24-in. (60-cm) lengths of pink dyed silk, approx. ¾–1½ in. (2–4 cm) wide

24 in. (60 cm) pink linked chain

2 fold-over crimps

2 x 7mm split rings

Lobster clasp

Pink filigree earring, approx. 1¼ in. (3 cm) in diameter

3 large chain links or jump rings

Door rosette, approx. 2 in. (5 cm) in diameter

3-in. (7.5-cm) bronze head pin

2 x 4mm bronze spacer beads

1 x 8mm pearl bead

Bow pin

## Tools

Beading mat

Jewelry glue

Toothpick to apply glue

Chain-, flat-, and round-nose pliers

Wire cutters

File

1 Lay the two strips of dyed silk and pink linked chain horizontally in front of you on a beading mat.

2 Using a toothpick, apply a small dab of glue to the center of the fold-over crimp. Insert the right-hand ends of the two pink silk strips into the crimp. Using flat-nose pliers, fold the sides of the crimp up and crimp as tightly as you can. Repeat on the left-hand side.

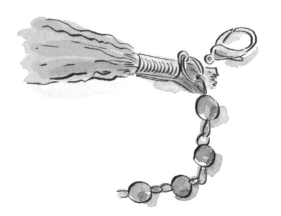

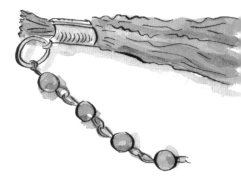

**3** Attach a split ring to the fold-over crimp loop and the last link of the pink linked chain on the right-hand end of the necklace. Repeat on the left-hand side, adding a lobster clasp to the split ring.

**4** Using wire cutters, cut the clip fastening or post from the back of the earring, cutting as close to the base as possible. File down any rough ridges and wipe clean (see page 15).

☞ If you have tintype photos or photos of your own, the door rosette makes a great frame for them.

5 Using large chain links, attach the earring to the silk-and-chain necklace, then attach the door rosette to the bottom of the earring.

6 Thread a 4mm spacer bead, an 8mm pearl bead, and another spacer bead onto the head pin. Using round-nose pliers, form the other end of the head pin into a wrapped loop (see page 15). Using a chain link, attach the pearl embellishment to the bottom of the door rosette.

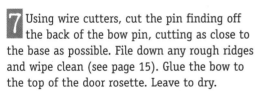

7 Using wire cutters, cut the pin finding off the back of the bow pin, cutting as close to the base as possible. File down any rough ridges and wipe clean (see page 15). Glue the bow to the top of the door rosette. Leave to dry.

# Butterfly Necklace

We don't always see the beauty of things in our everyday lives, but if we open our eyes and use our imagination we can transform even the most mundane of objects into something extraordinary. In this design, an metal hinge metamorphoses into a butterfly!

## Materials

Butterfly hinge

Three 9-in. (23-cm) lengths of chain

4 x 14mm jump rings

One 16-in. (40-cm) length of chain

Clasp

4 jump rings for charms

Embellishments of your choice: I used a cross, flower cabochon, crown with bronze patina, crystal charm, flower charm, and watch fob tag

## Tools

Beading mat

Chain- and flat-nose pliers

Jewelry glue

Toothpick

**1** Using the 14mm jump rings, attach two 9-in. (23-cm) lengths of chain to the top hole on the left-hand side of the butterfly hinge and one 9-in. (23-cm) length to the top hole of the right-hand side.

**2** Attach a 14mm jump ring and one end of the 16-in. (40-cm) chain to the end of the right-hand chain. Attach a 14mm jump ring, the other end of the 16-in. (40-cm) chain, and a clasp to the ends of the two left-hand chains.

**3** Using a toothpick, apply an appropriate amount of jewelry glue to the center of the cross, then attach the flower cabochon to the cross. Leave to dry.

4 Using jump rings, attach your chosen embellishments to the center of the 16-in. (40-cm) chain.

# Chapter 4

# Family Treasures

In this chapter I have tried to use relics
that are often passed from generation to
generation. Rescue your own personal
treasures from their hiding place in an
old jewelry box and use them to create
treasured heirlooms to pass down to your
loved ones.

# Watch Soul Earrings

Ladies' watches were once an elegant style statement, but are now often left unworking in a jewelry box. This delicate design of re-purposed watch plates gives old souls a new life.

## Materials

2 x ladies' vintage watches

2 x 9mm rosette cabochons

2 x 2-in. (5-cm) eye pins

2 x 8mm pearl bead

2 x ear wires

2 x 6mm crystal beads

2 x 2-in. (5-cm) head pins

## Tools

Small flat-head screwdriver

Jewelry glue

Beading mat

Chain-, flat-, and round-nose pliers

Wire cutters

1 Prise off the backs of the two vintage watches; you will need a small flat-head screwdriver to do this. Inside each one, you will find a small metal plate that holds the watch workings; this is what I call the "watch soul."

2 Set the two "watch souls" in front of you on your beading mat, both facing in the same direction, and decide which is the top and bottom. I place the best center hole at the top. Apply a tiny amount of jewelry glue to the center of each watch soul and attach a rosette cabochon. Leave to dry.

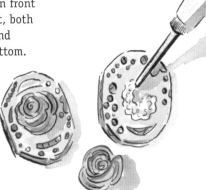

*"Lost time is never found again."*

Benjamin Franklin

3 Thread each pearl onto an eye pin. Using wire cutters, cut the pins ⅜ in. (1 cm) below the pearls. Using round-nose pliers, curl the cut end of each eye pin into a semi-circle that faces the same way as the original eye. Thread a watch soul onto each one, then complete the loop.

☞ Vintage watches are great finds at thrift stores and garage sales; don't worry about the condition, because you will only be using the inside "souls." And don't be afraid to steer away from symmetry and use mis-matched watch plates for a sassy touch.

4 Using chain-nose pliers, open the loop at the base of each ear wire in turn. Thread on the pearl bead and watch soul, making sure that the rosette cabochon is facing outward, then close the loop.

5 Thread a crystal bead onto each head pin. Cut the pin ⅜ in. (1 cm) above the bead. Using round-nose pliers, curl the cut end of each eye pin into a semi-circle. Hook the semi-circle over the hole at the bottom of the watch soul, then close the loop with your round-nose pliers.

# His & Hers Earrings

Tintypes were first developed in France in 1853 and were incredibly popular throughout the 19th century as an inexpensive form of portrait. Here the "his and hers" portraits, perhaps of a married couple, make a charming pair of earrings.

## Materials

2 tintype photos, approx. 1 x ¾ in. (2.5 x 2 cm)

2 x 6mm jump rings

2 x 4-ring strand connectors

4 x 3mm crystal beads

4 x 2-in. (5-cm) head pins

8 x 3mm flat-backed crystals

2 ear wires

## Tools

Wooden block

Safety pin and spray sealant

Beading mat

Chain-, flat-, and round-nose pliers

Wire cutters

Toothpick

Jewelry glue

Tweezers

**1** Lay the tintype photos on a wooden block and spray with spray sealant. Leave to dry. (The sealant helps prevent the surface from getting scratched.) Using a safety pin, make a hole in the center top of both tintypes.

**2** Using a 6mm jump ring, attach one tintype photo to the center hole of each 4-ring strand connector (see page 14).

*"I am his beloved and he is mine."*

Song of Solomon.

**3** Thread a crystal bead onto a head pin, then cut the head pin ¼ in. (5mm) above the bead. Using round-nose pliers, curl the cut end of the head pin into a semi-circle (see page 14). Hook the semi-circle over one of the bottom holes of the 4-ring strand connector, then close the semi-circle. Repeat with the remaining crystal beads.

**4** Using round-nose pliers, open the loop at the base of one ear wire, hook it through the loop at the top of one 4-ring strand connector, and close it again. Repeat with the second ear wire.

**5** Using a toothpick, apply a tiny dab of glue to each corner of one tintype. Using tweezers, pick up a flat-backed crystal and in place at each spot. Repeat with the second tintype.

☞ To take this design further, add charms stamped with sayings such as his/hers; boy/girl; mom/dad; or I/Do on wedding photographs.

# Heirloom Pin

Both masculine and feminine in its design, this heirloom-inspired pin can be worn by everyone. It allows you to bring diverse family pieces out of the jewelry box, combining unique and eclectic treasures into one design and giving them new meaning.

## Materials

Vintage retractable pin with base loop

Rhinestone connector

Vintage or heirloom-style embellishments of your choice: I used a "Pop" pocket knife, clock hand, bronze cross, watch face, and pearl button

14mm chain links or jump rings

4 x 8mm jump rings

3-in. (7.5-cm) pin

6mm faceted crystal bead

2 x 6mm crimp bead covers

2-in. (5-cm) length of beaded chain

## Tools

Wire cutters

File

Beading mat

Chain- and flat-nose pliers

**1** If necessary, use wire cutters to snip off any posts or findings from the back of your embellishments, file smooth, and wipe clean (see page 17).

**2** Attach the top loop of the rhinestone connector to the base loop of the vintage pin. Attach a 14mm chain link to the other loop of the rhinestone connector.

**3** Attach a 14mm chain link to the top loop of the pocket knife. Connect the pocket knife to the chain link at the base of the rhinestone connector via an additional chain link. Attach the clock hand to the pin via one more chain link.

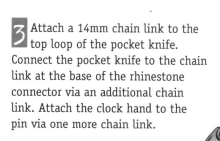

**4** Using the tip of your round-nose pliers, form a small wrapped loop (see page 15) at the end of the 3-in. (7.5-cm) pin. Thread a 6mm faceted crystal bead onto the open end of the pin and push the bead up against the wrapped loop. Thread the watch face embellishment onto the wire, bend the wire up, and form a wrapped loop below the crystal bead. Cover the wrapped wires with crimp bead covers (see page 15).

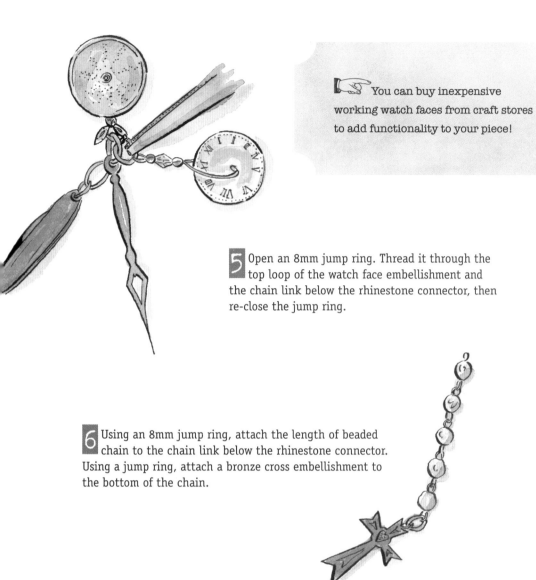

☞ You can buy inexpensive working watch faces from craft stores to add functionality to your piece!

5 Open an 8mm jump ring. Thread it through the top loop of the watch face embellishment and the chain link below the rhinestone connector, then re-close the jump ring.

6 Using an 8mm jump ring, attach the length of beaded chain to the chain link below the rhinestone connector. Using a jump ring, attach a bronze cross embellishment to the bottom of the chain.

7 Open a small jump ring, loop it through the shank on the back of the pearl button, then close the jump ring again. Attach the button to the chain link below the rhinestone connector via a second jump ring.

# Framed Tintype Necklace

The top hat has been the definitive symbol of high fashion and sophistication throughout the decades. Look for similar photographs that are packed with history and are worthy to be framed, or use this method to showcase your own.

## Materials

2½ x 1¾-in. (6 x 4.5-cm) brass patina frame

2 x 12-in. (30-cm) lengths of chain

2 x 1½-in. (5 x 4-cm) tintype photo

4 x 5mm jump rings

Lobster clasp

1 x 3-in. (7.5-cm) eye pin

1 x 12mm pearl bead

Small watch piece

1 x 6mm crimp bead

2½ x 1¾-in. (6 x 4.5-cm) cloth for backing

## Tools

Beading mat

Wooden block

Marker pen

Center punch

Drill and ¹⁄₁₆-in. (1.5mm) drill bit

Chain-, flat-, and round-nose pliers

Scissors

Jewelry glue

**1** Lay the brass patina frame on a wooden block and make a small indentation with a center punch in the upper left and right corners. Drill a ¹⁄₁₆-in. (1.5-mm) hole at each point.

2 Using 5mm jump rings, attach one 12-in. (30-cm) length of chain to each hole (see page 14).

3 Attach a 5mm jump ring to the end of the right-hand chain and a 5mm jump ring and lobster clasp to the end of the left-hand chain.

👉 You can often find mini frames and other great pieces in the scrapbook section of craft stores; age the brass yourself using a patina solution (see page 17).

**4** Thread a pearl bead onto the eye pin, pushing it right up against the eye. Using the center of your round-nose pliers, starting ½ in. (1 cm) from the base of the pearl bead make the beginning of a wrapped loop. Thread the watch piece onto the wired pin and complete the wrapped loop. Cut off the excess pin wire.

**5** Cover the wrapped loop with a crimp bead cover (see page 15).

**6** Using round-nose pliers, open the eye of the eye pin and attach the pearl-and-watch charm to the right-hand length of chain 1 in. (2.5 cm) above the top of the frame.

**7** If necessary, trim the tintype photo with scissors so that all the edges are behind the frame. Using jewelry glue, stick the photo to the back of the frame. Turn the frame over. Using jewelry glue, stick a small piece of fabric over the back of the frame to cover the photo.

# Grandma's Necklace

Jewelry and trinkets often carry with them special memories of the person who first owned them, stories passed on from generation to generation. Showcase these treasured possessions and wear them close to your heart.

## Materials

2 x 10-in. (5–25-cm) peach crystal linked chains

1 x 10-in. (25-cm) strand of pearl linked chain

1 x 6mm and 3 x 12mm jump rings

Lobster clasp

5–7 short lengths of large-linked chain

Embellishments of your choice: I used a pearl earring, two pearl monogrammed heart scarf clips, pearl button, crystal bead, good luck charm, gold earring

## Tools

Beading mat

Chain-, flat-, and round-nose pliers

Wire cutters

File

**1** Open a 6mm jump ring, thread on the two peach crystal linked chains and then the pearl linked chain, then close the jump ring. Open a 12mm jump ring, thread it through the jump ring that links the three chains together, then close the jump ring again. This makes the center ring of the necklace from which you will hang the cluster of "treasures."

**2** Attach a 12mm jump ring to the end of the pearl beaded chain and close. Attach a 12 mm jump ring and a lobster clasp to the ends of the two peach beaded chain ends and close.

☞ The center cluster of this piece would also look great on a long chain. Alternatively, make it fun and funky using children's charms!

**3** If necessary, use wire cutters to snip off any backing posts or findings from your vintage embellishment, file smooth, and wipe clean (see page 17).

**4** Attach the required number of lengths of chain to the center ring; I used five lengths—one for each charm. Using jump rings, attach your chosen "treasures" to the center ring or to individual chain links in whatever order you choose, varying the height at which they hang to create an attractive-looking cluster.

# Time Flies Necklace

Pocket watches, worn with grandeur by our forefathers, are a testament to detail and quality craftsmanship that is often forgotten. Refashioned into a unique upcycled piece of jewelry, you can now have a way to showcase these forgotten heirlooms. Working or not, they make a stunning statement with a story to tell.

## Materials

Pocket watch approx. 2½ in. (6 cm) in diameter

4 x 5mm, 3 x 8mm, and 4 x 10mm jump rings

2 x 18mm gold-colored flower connector charms

16-in. (40-cm) beaded necklace

Box clasp

Embellishments: copper dove, small key, watch gear

## Tools

Beading mat

Chain- and flat-nose pliers

**1** Attach two 5mm jump rings to the top loop of the pocket watch (see page 14). Using two 10mm jump rings, attach one gold-colored flower connector charm to each 5mm jump ring.

**2** Lay the beaded necklace horizontally in front of you on the beading mat. Using an 8mm jump ring, attach one end of the necklace to the top loop of the right-hand flower connecter charm.

*"The only reason for time is so that everything doesn't happen at once."*

Albert Einstein

This design also looks great made with chain or ribbon as the necklace base. Adding whimsical-looking charms counterbalances the more masculine style of the pocket watch.

**3** Using an 8mm jump ring, attach the other end of the beaded necklace to one side of the box clasp. Then use another 8mm jump ring to attach the other side of the box clasp to the top of the left-hand connector charm.

**4** Attach the copper dove to the jump ring below the right-hand connector charm, using two 5mm jump rings linked together. Use two individual 10mm jump rings to attach the key and watch gear embellishments to the jump ring below the left-hand connector charm in the same way.

# Father Necklace

Use this design to make a necklace that signifies a time or memory you have with your dad. You don't have to use heirloom pieces for the embellishments: it's what the embellishments remind you of that's important. Fishing lures to signify that special trip on the lake, washers and tattered pieces of rags to remind you of your first lesson in oil change—anything goes!

## Materials

4 embellishments of your choice: I used a pocket knife, photo button, lighter, and aged brass button

24 in. (60 cm) large-linked, aged bronzed chain

4 x 7mm jump rings

2 x 8-10 mm chain links

Lobster clasp

12 mm connector bead

## Tools

Beading mat

Wire cutters

File

Chain-, flat-, and round-nose pliers

**1** If necessary, use wire cutters to snip off any posts or findings from the back of your vintage embellishments, file down any rough ridges, and wipe clean (see page 17). If you're using a vintage pin, cut the straight pin ⅜ in. (1 cm) from the end and form it into a loop using round-nose pliers (see page 14).

**2** Attach a 7mm jump ring to the right-hand end of the large-linked aged bronze chain and a 7mm jump ring and a lobster clasp to the left-hand end (see page 14).

**3** Find the center of the large-linked aged bronze chain. Using a 7mm jump ring, attach the lighter 1 in. (2.5 cm) to the left of the center, then clip the clasp of the lighter chain higher up the large-linked chain, allowing some slack. (The lighter that I used in this necklace was already attached to a chain, with a hoop clasp at the end; if your chosen embellishment is not, you will need to add a chain and clasp.)

**4** My pocket knife was also attached to chain. Using a 7mm jump ring, attach the pocket knife to the center of the large-linked chain, allowing a 3-in. (7.5-cm) drop. Using a 7mm jump ring or the clasp (if there is one) on the chain end, attach the other end of the pocket knife chain to last but one link of the large chain. (Again, you will need to add a chain and clasp if the knife does not already have one.)

☞ Watch fobs, pocket watches, and old buttons are all great relics to use in creating this necklace. Find pieces with their existing chain still attached and incorporate them into the design to add interest and layering.

**5** Attach the photo button to the base of a 12mm connector bead and a 10mm chain link to the top. Using an 8mm jump ring, attach the top of the connector bead to the center link of the large chain.

**6** Using a 7mm jump ring, attach the aged brass button to the right-hand side of the large chain, 2 in. (5 cm) from the center.

# Expressions Necklace

I love the expressions that are often caught by accident on old photos. The long exposures needed to take a photo usually mean that the sitters are not smiling, so finding a candid shot like this one is like finding a diamond in the rough.

## Materials

3 x 2½-in. (7.5 x 6-cm) tintype photo

2¾ x 1¾-in. (7 x 4.5-cm) number tag

Large chain links

2 x 12-in. (30-cm) lengths of beaded chain

3 x 7mm jump rings

Lobster clasp

2 x 14mm pearl beads

2 x 3-in. (5–7.5-cm) eye pins

3½-in. (9-cm) length of snake chain

Round ¾-in. (2-cm) copper stamping blank

2 x 8mm black Swarovski crystals

## Tools

Beading mat

Chain-, flat-, and round-nose pliers

Spray sealant

Marker pen

Scissors

Jewelry glue

Toothpick

Two-hole screw-down jewelry punch

Steel block and hammer

Metal stamps

Patina solution

Cotton bud

Heavy-duty scouring pad

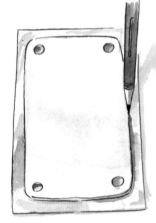

**1** Following the manufacturer's instructions, spray your tintype photo with sealant to prevent any damage during wear.

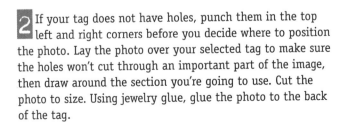

**2** If your tag does not have holes, punch them in the top left and right corners before you decide where to position the photo. Lay the photo over your selected tag to make sure the holes won't cut through an important part of the image, then draw around the section you're going to use. Cut the photo to size. Using jewelry glue, glue the photo to the back of the tag.

3 Using a two-hole screw-down jewelry punch, punch holes through the holes in the top of the tag, making sure your photo is the right way up.

4 Using large chain links, attach one 12-in. (30-cm) chain length to each side of the tag. Attach a jump ring to the end of the right-hand chain and a jump ring and a lobster clasp to the end of the left-hand chain.

5 Thread a pearl bead onto an eye pin, pushing it right up against the eye. Using wire cutters, cut the stem of the pin ⅜ in. (1 cm) above the bead. Using round-nose pliers, curl the cut end of the stem into a loop to form another eye, making sure it faces the same way as the original eye. Repeat with the second pearl bead and eye pin.

6 Open a link in the chain 3 in. (7.5 cm) above the photo tag on each side of the necklace. Using round-nose pliers, open the eye loops of one pearl bead, hook into each end of the disconnected chain, and close the eyes again. Repeat with the second pearl bead on the other side of the necklace.

**7** Using 7mm jump rings, attach one end of the snake chain to the bottom eye of each pearl bead.

**8** Lay the copper blank flat on a steel block. Holding each metal stamp vertically, tap the top with the hammer to stamp your chosen word or phrase letter by letter.

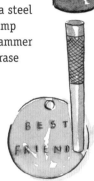

**9** Using a cotton bud, apply patina solution copper blank until you get the shade you want (see page 17).

**10** Using a heavy-duty scouring pad, scrub the surface patina from the copper blank until only the letters remain blackened. Rinse with water, then dry the blank.

**11** Open a 7mm jump ring, loop it through the hole in the top of the copper blank and over the snake chain, then close the jump ring again.

**12** Using a toothpick, apply a small dab of jewelry glue to the holes at the bottom of the tag (if it has holes) and attach large Swarovski crystals to cover. Leave to dry.

# Time on Your Hands Cuff

This statement cuff is made of mixed materials and laced with elegance and can be worn as a daily reminder of just how precious each moment in time is.

## Materials

Strip of black leather, 1½ in. (4 cm) wide and approx. 6 in. (15 cm) long

Clock face

36-in. (90-cm) length of silk, approx. ½ in. (12 mm) wide

Flat-backed 7mm crystal

Silk scraps

6mm Swarovski crystal

10mm pearl bead

## Tools

Leather punch

Wooden block

Marker pen

Drill and ¹⁄₁₆-in. (1.5-mm) drill bit

File

Needle

Quilting thread

Jewelry glue

Toothpick

**1** Using a leather punch set to a ⅛-in. (3-mm) hole, punch three evenly spaced holes along each short end of the leather strip.

**2** Decide where you want to drill holes in the clock face to attach it to the leather, then mark these points with a marker pen.

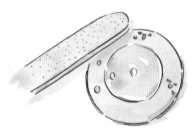

**3** Lay the clock face on a wooden block and make a small indentation with a center punch at the marked points. Drill ¹⁄₁₆-in. (1.5-mm) holes at each point. Turn the clock face over and file the area around the holes to smooth the edges (see page 16).

**4** Using a needle and quilting thread, which is stronger than ordinary sewing thread, stitch the right-hand side of the clock face to the center of the leather band. I stitched in a scrap of silk as an embellishment at the same time. Tie the thread in a knot on the back of the leather strip and trim off any excess.

**5** Stitch the left-hand side of the clock face to the leather strip in the same way, attaching a 6mm Swarovski crystal and pearl bead as you sew. Tie the thread in a knot on the back of the leather strip and trim off any excess.

**6** Using a toothpick, apply a tiny amount of jewelry glue over the thread knots on the back of the leather strip for extra security.

**7** Using a toothpick, apply a tiny amount of jewelry glue to the center of the clock face and stick on a flat-backed crystal.

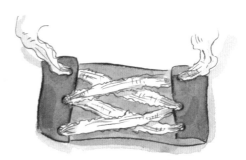

8 Thread the length of silk in a crisscross pattern through the holes on the leather strip, leaving the same amount protruding at each end so that you can tie the strip around your wrist.

☞ You can prolong the life of your leather punch by placing a scrap piece of leather under the leather you are punching, so that you do not scar the punch tips.

# Mother Necklace

Mothers are always leaving us bits of advice and little mementos along the way. In this design you can create a piece using those mementos. This necklace harks back to the romantic days of formal balls, when a gentleman would request the pleasure of a dance from his sweetheart by inscribing his name on her dance card with a small pencil such as the one in this design.

## Materials

6 embellishments of your choice:
I used a mother-of-pearl pin,
a mechanical dance pencil, a
photo button, a brass button,
a brass keyhole fitting, and a
cameo earring

28-in. (71-cm) gold-and-pearl
necklace

8mm jump rings

2-in. (5-cm) head pin

9mm pearl bead

6mm crystal bead

3-in. (7.5-cm) eye pin (optional)

9mm bead connector

Lobster clasp

## Tools

Beading mat

Chain-, flat-, and round-nose pliers

Wire cutters

File

**1** If necessary, use wire cutters to snip off any posts or findings from the back of your embellishments, file down any rough ridges, and wipe clean (see page 17).

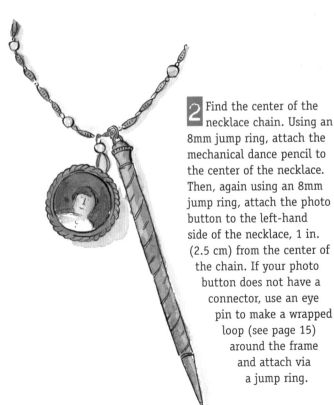

**2** Find the center of the necklace chain. Using an 8mm jump ring, attach the mechanical dance pencil to the center of the necklace. Then, again using an 8mm jump ring, attach the photo button to the left-hand side of the necklace, 1 in. (2.5 cm) from the center of the chain. If your photo button does not have a connector, use an eye pin to make a wrapped loop (see page 15) around the frame and attach via a jump ring.

**3** Close the fastener hook on the back of the mother-of-pearl pin with your round-nose pliers. Using wire cutters, cut the straight pin ³⁄₈ in. (1 cm) from the hinge, then curl the wire into the loop with your round-nose pliers (see page 14).

**4** Using an 8mm jump ring, attach the mother-of-pearl pin to the right-hand side of the necklace, 1 in. (2.5 cm) from the center of the chain.

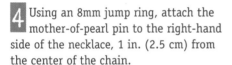

**5** Thread a 9mm pearl bead and a 6mm crystal bead onto a head pin, then form the other end of the head pin into a wrapped loop (see page 15). Using an 8mm jump ring, attach the pearl/crystal combination to the bottom loop of the mother-of-pearl pin.

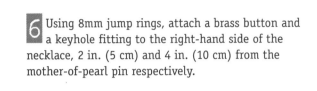

6 Using 8mm jump rings, attach a brass button and a keyhole fitting to the right-hand side of the necklace, 2 in. (5 cm) and 4 in. (10 cm) from the mother-of-pearl pin respectively.

7 Using an 8mm jump ring, attach a cameo earring to a bead connector, then attach the bead connector to the right-hand side of the necklace, 2 in. (5 cm) from the keyhole fitting. Add a jump ring to one end of the necklace chain and a jump ring and lobster clasp to the other.

# Embellishments Necklace

Guaranteed to catch anyone's eye, this necklace combines a selection of earrings and brooches in a sophisticated design that will allow you to stand out from the crowd.

**1** Arrange the brooches and earrings in your choice of order on your beading mat.

**2** If necessary, use wire cutters to snip off any posts or findings from the back of your embellishments, file down any rough ridges, and wipe clean (see page 17). Leave the shanks on the backs of the buttons.

(see page 17)

## Materials

5 assorted brooches and earrings

2 buttons with shanks on the back

11 jump rings or chain links

10 in. (25 cm) of linked chain

Lobster clasp

## Tools

Beading mat

Wire cutters

File

Chain- and flat-nose pliers

**3** Using jumps rings or large chain links, join the pieces together using the original holes. (Depending on the size and shape of the pieces, it's often a good idea to connect the pieces together at two points on each side, as this will make it easier for the necklace to lie nice and flat.)

**4** Using jump rings or chain links, attach the desired length of chain to each end of the necklace. I added 4 in. (10 cm) to each end.

Attach a large jump ring to the end of the right-hand chain and a large jump ring and a lobster clasp to the end of the left-hand chain.

☞ Making this necklace is a true treasure hunt! Look for pieces with filigree and original holes, as this will make it easier to assemble the necklace.

# Suppliers

Hunting for your own treasures is part of the fun and checking out local garage sales, thrift stores, and online auctions is a great way to make some shopping steals. My favorite finds are at flea market or antiquing venues: you might pay a little more for the item but they are easier to find and, if you're lucky, the vendor might have a story to go with it. And if you just can't wait or don't want to spend the time on the road, you can shop at eBay and Etsy from anywhere and at any time across the world.

In addition to specialty jewelry stores, good craft stores have all kinds of things that you can incorporate into your jewelry designs. Check out the scrapbooking sections, in particular, for vintage-style decorative items such as tags and miniature frames. Above all, don't forget that you can create really imaginative, one-of-a-kind pieces of jewelry using anything that takes your fancy. For this reason, I've also listed some nationwide home improvement stores, because they can be great sources of small items of domestic hardware such as keys and keyhole covers, as well as tools.

## US

**Craft and jewelry supply stores**

**Fire Mountain Gems**
www.firemountaingems.com

**Hobby Lobby**
www.hobbylobby.com

**Jo-Ann Fabric & Craft Stores**
www.joann.com

**Rio Grande**
www.riogrande.com

**Home improvement stores**

**Ace Hardware**
www.acehardware.com

**Harbor Freight**
www.harborfreight.com

**The Home Depot**
www.homedepot.com

**Lowes**
www.lowes.com

## UK

**Craft and jewelry supply stores**

**The Bead Shop**
www.beadworks.co.uk

**Craft Superstore**
www.craftsuperstore.co.uk

**Creative Beadcraft**
www.creativebeadcraft.co.uk

**Hobbycraft**
www.hobbycraft.co.uk

**Home improvement stores**

**B&Q**
www.diy.com

**Homebase**
www.homebase.co.uk

**Wickes**
www.wickes.co.uk

# Index

# Acknowledgments

I would like to thank everyone at CICO Books for crossing my path and giving me this wonderful adventure. It was my first time to get to travel this road.

My great support system—Denise McDonald, Amy Kleinwachter, Jana McCann, Cindi Starr, and Teresa McDonald—for taking my phone calls, listening, believing, and accepting me the way I am.

Thank you to my treasure hunters, Dixie Chatham of Dixie's Den of Antiquities, Kindra Weston of Weston Primitive Co., and Brian Kleinwachter of Old World Antieks.

And to my loving husband Vince and son Kyler, who tolerated the million ideas I had flying across the house at all hours. I appreciate you and adore you.

To Mom and Dad, all four brothers, my favorite sister, and the so many people who have made me the creative soul that I am and supported my efforts.

And to My Lord and Savior, I give you my All.